North American Indians Today

North American Indians Today

Apache

Cherokee

Cheyenne

Comanche

Creek

Crow

Huron

Iroquois

Navajo

Ojibwa

Osage

Potawatomi

Pueblo

Seminole

Sioux

North American
Indians Today

Sioux

by
Karen LoneHill

Mason Crest Publishers

Philadelphia

The authors wish to thank the people who helped with this book: Brian Patterson, Birdy Burdeck, Kay Olan, Jessica Howard, Mark Emery, and Mike Tarbell.

Mason Crest Publishers Inc.
370 Reed Road
Broomall, Pennsylvania 19008
(866) MCP-BOOK (toll free)

First printing
1 2 3 4 5 6 7 8 9 10
Library of Congress Cataloging-in-Publication Data on file at the Library of Congress.
ISBN: 1-59084-678-8
1-59084-663-X (series)

Design by Lori Holland.
Composition by Bytheway Publishing Services, Binghamton, New York.
Cover design by Benjamin Stewart.
Printed and bound in the Hashemite Kingdom of Jordan.

Photography by Benjamin Stewart. Pictures on pp. 34, 45, are used courtesy of Russell Maylone, curator of Northwestern University Library; picture on p. 62 is courtesy of Vanessa Shortbull; pp. 69, 70 courtesy of Viola Ruelke Gommer. Pictures on pp. 6, 47, 60 are by Keith Rosco.

Contents

Why is it so important that Indians be brought into the "mainstream" of American life?
I would not know how to interpret this phrase to my people.
The closest I would be able to come would be "a big wide river".
Am I then to tell my people that they are to be thrown into the big, wide river of the United States?

Earl Old Person
Blackfeet Tribal Chairman

Introduction

In the midst of twenty-first–century North America, how do the very first North Americans hold on to their unique cultural identity? At the same time, how do they adjust to the real demands of the modern world? Earl Old Person's quote on the opposite page expresses the difficulty of achieving this balance. Even the common values of the rest of North America—like fitting into the "mainstream"—may seem strange or undesireable to North American Indians. How can these groups of people thrive and prosper in the twenty-first century without losing their traditions, the ways of thinking and living that have been handed down to them by their ancestors? How can they keep from drowning in North America's "big, wide river"?

Thoughts from the Series Consultant

Each of the books in this series was written with the help of Native scholars and tribal leaders from the particular tribe. Based on oral histories as well as written documents, these books describe the current strategies of each Native nation to develop its economy while maintaining strong ties with its culture. As a result, you may find that these books read far differently from other books about Native Americans.

Over the past centuries, Native groups have faced increasing pressure to conform to the wishes of the governments that took their lands. Often brutally inhumane methods were implemented to change Native social systems. These books describe the ways that Native groups refused to be passive recipients of change, even in the face of these past atrocities. Heroic individuals worked to fit external changes into local conditions. This struggle continues today.

The legacy of the past still haunts the psyche of both Native and non-Native people of North America; hopefully, these books will help correct some misunderstandings. And even with the difficulties encountered by past and current Native leaders, Native nations continue to thrive. As this series illustrates, Native populations continue to increase—and they have clearly persevered against incredible odds. North American culture's big, wide river may be deep and cold—but Native Americans are good swimmers!

—*Martha McCollough*

Breaking Stereotypes

One way that some North Americans may "drown" Native culture is by using stereotypes to think about North American Indians. When we use stereotypes to think about a group of people, we assume things about them because of their race or cultural group. Instead of taking time to understand individual differences and situations, we lump together everyone in a certain group. In reality, though, every person is different. More than two million Native people live in North America, and they are as *diverse* as any other group. Each one is unique.

Even if we try hard to avoid stereotypes, however, it isn't always easy to know what words to use. Should we call the people who are native to North America Native Americans—or American Indians—or just Indians?

The word "Indian" probably comes from a mistake—when Christopher Columbus arrived in the New World, he thought he had reached India, so he called the people he found there Indians. Some people feel it doesn't make much sense to call Native Americans "Indians." (Suppose Columbus had thought he landed in China instead of India; would we today call Native people "Chinese"?) Other scholars disagree; for example, Russell Means, Native politician and activist, claims that the word "Indian" comes from Columbus saying the native people were *en Dios*—"in God," or naturally spiritual.

Many Canadians use the term "First Nations" to refer to the Native peoples who live there, and people in the United States usually speak of Native Americans. Most Native people we talked to while we were writing these books prefer the simple term "Indian"—or they would rather use the names of their tribes. (We have used the term "North American Indians" for our series to distinguish this group of people from the inhabitants of India.)

Even the definition of what makes a person "Indian" varies. The U.S. government recognizes certain groups as tribal nations (almost 500 in all). Each nation then decides how it will enroll people as members of that tribe. Tribes may require a particular amount of Indian blood, tribal membership of the father or the mother, or other *criteria*. Some enrolled tribal members who are legally "Indian" may not look Native at all; many have blond hair and blue eyes and others have clearly African features. At the same time, there are thousands of Native people whose tribes have not yet been officially recognized by the government.

We have done our best to write books that are as free from stereotypes as possible. But you as the reader also play a part. After reading one of these books, we hope you won't think: "The Cheyenne are all like this" or "Iroquois are all like that." Each person in this world is unique, whatever their culture. Stereotypes shut people's minds—but these books are intended to open your mind. North American Indians today have much wisdom and beauty to offer.

Some people consider American Indians to be a historical topic only, but Indians today are living, contributing members of North American society. The contributions of the various Indian cultures enrich our world—and North America would be a very different place without the Native people who live there. May they never be lost in North America's "big, wide river"!

Long before Mt. Rushmore was carved with the faces of U.S. presidents, the Black Hills were the sacred lands of the Oceti Sakowin people.

Chapter 1

Oral Traditions

Thousands of tourists travel to the Black Hills of South Dakota each summer to visit Mount Rushmore, the nation's Shrine of Democracy. It represents freedom for all Americans, but at the same time the Black Hills represent a culture's connection to the world and universe. Each year, students from the outlying *reservation* schools and tribal colleges travel into this area to visit the various sites to understand the oral traditions that have been passed down from the past generations.

Rock art in the form of *petroglyphs* and *pictographs* dating from 2500 B.C. to 1850 A.D. in the Black Hills has inspired considerable interest in the remote history and culture of the Oceti Sakowin—the Sioux. Imagine walking through the serene, tree-lined canyons, wondering what the stories on the walls meant to a people eons ago. One petroglyph, for instance, depicted images of a possible hunt: buffalo, elk, men on foot holding spears (this was long before the time of the bow and arrow and the acquisition of the horse). A petroglyph on another wall reveals a possible prehistoric animal battling with humans. And yet another wall shows a pictograph that some people argue could be a UFO—but most **anthropologists** agree is a map of some sort.

The creators of these drawings left no written records to explain their work. Recording a symbol on a hide was the closest that this culture came to writing their tribal history. Instead, they handed down stories, from one generation to another. These oral traditions are still important to the Sioux people today. The stories describe the Sioux's earliest history—and many tell of a time before humans, when the earth was just forming.

In the beginning, Inyan (rock) existed and his spirit was Wakan Tanka (the Great Mystery); he was soft and supple, and his blood was blue. Han (night) also existed, but she was not a being, only the darkness. Being alone, Inyan desired others, so he created a disk that he called Maka

An ancient petroglyph is carved at Medicine Rock, Montana, a site sacred to the Cheyenne and Oceti Sakowin.

(earth). As he took so much from himself, his veins opened, and all his blood flowed. He shrank and became hard. His blood became Mni (blue waters) upon Maka. The powers separated, and Mahpiyato (great blue dome-sky) surrounded Maka.

Today, one of the Sioux's seven sacred ceremonies, the Inipi (sweat lodge), reflects the importance of this oral tradition by using stones and water to purify the mind and body. In the sweat lodge, honor and respect are bestowed on the beginning of time.

According to Sioux *Ohunkakan* (creation stories) and tribal tradition, the Sioux originated within the Black Hills themselves. The story goes back to a time in history when the Sioux lived underground beneath the hills. Eventually, they were enticed to the surface of the earth, emerging through Wind Cave in the southern Black Hills.

Waziya, the old man from the north, and his wife Wakanka had been banished to the surface of the earth for an earlier misdeed and now longed for human company. So, along with Iktomi, the spider trickster, they schemed a way to lure humans to the surface. Iktomi instructed them to prepare food, berries, and beautiful clothing of tanned deer hides; they were to wait at the opening for glimpses of the people. Waziya and his wife would tell the people that these items were abundant above ground and could be theirs if they came to the surface.

Full of curiosity, one young man disregarded the advice of his leader and led his followers to the surface. He was known as Tokahe, "the first." Once the people had emerged, they were unable to return to the place that had been their home for thousands of years—and they realized they had been deceived by Waziya, Wakanka, and Iktomi. Their leader, whom they had left behind underground, foresaw the fate of his people and the hardships they would encounter. He sacrificed his safe existence and came to the surface in the form of a buffalo. The buffalo sustained the people during that early period; it provided food, clothing, shelter, tools—all the necessities of life.

The Oceti Sakowin's connection between the earth and the constellations is told through many stories that fall under the category of Ohunkakan (creation stories). One story is that of Fallen Star.

Long ago, there were two young women who were lying outside of their tepee, looking at the stars. It was a beautiful, clear summer night. One wished to marry the bright star, and the other wished to marry the dimmer

WIND CAVE NATURAL ENTRANCE

THE SMALL HOLE BELOW MARKS THE SITE OF THE ORIGINAL
CAVE OPENING DISCOVERED BY TOM BINGHAM IN 1881. A
WHISTLING SOUND AND WAVING GRASSES AND BUSHES NEARBY
ATTRACTED HIS ATTENTION AS HE PASSED BY.

CHANGING ATMOSPHERIC PRESSURE OUTSIDE THE CAVE CAUSES
THE AIR INSIDE THE CAVE TO ADJUST. WHEN THE PRESSURE
OUTSIDE THE CAVE RISES, THE AIR OUTSIDE ENTERS THE CAVE
THROUGH ANY OPENINGS; WHEN THE PRESSURE OUTSIDE THE
CAVE FALLS, AIR LEAVES THE CAVE. CAVE AIR ADJUSTING TO
THE OUTSIDE PRESSURE CAUSES THE WIND FOR WHICH THE
CAVE WAS NAMED.

Wind Cave, in the southern Black Hills, is the place where sacred traditions say the Oceti Sakowin emerged into this world.

Bear Butte in South Dakota is an ancient holy place that the Lakota call He Wakinyan Hohpi, which means Thunder Nest Mountain. He Wakinyan Hohpi is home to Wakinyan, the first Thunder-Being, who is also called a Thunder-Bird. Wakinyan represents cleansing; when he storms, Wakinyan is cleansing the earth so that the plants may live. Bear Butte is now a state park, where it is not always easy to balance the needs of Native people who worship there with the demands of tourists at the site.

star. They eventually fell asleep. When the women awoke, they found themselves in the sky—among the star people. Their wishes had come true. One of the young women married the bright star, who was an older man, and the other married the dim star, who was the younger man. One of the women became pregnant. One day they were overcome with homesickness and longed for the days when they dug turnips and gathered berries with their women relatives. Their husbands were preparing for a journey and, sensing the women's restlessness, warned them not to dig a particular turnip.

On their outing, inquisitiveness and defiance overcame the pregnant

The bison provided food, shelter, and practically all the necessities of life for Plains Indians. Anglo-American hunters drove the bison almost to extinction at the same time they were trying to destroy Native cultures in the American West.

woman and, against the pleading of her friend, she dug the forbidden turnip. It created a hole that pulled her in . . . and she fell back down to the earth. She didn't survive the fall, but her belly split open, giving life to her baby son.

The birds were the first to come upon this baby boy, and they held a council to decide what action was to be taken. They all spoke, each excusing itself from involvement, except for the Meadowlark, who took the child under her care and protection.

The child grew at a miraculous rate. When he became a young man, the Meadowlark instructed him to go to a nearby village. He was to approach a tepee on the edge of the encampment where an elderly woman lived and introduce himself as Wicahpi Hinhpaya (Fallen Star). This he did and joined his mother's people. He was an extraordinary person who later performed many courageous feats in defense of his human relatives.

This story is still told by the Sioux to teach values and morals. The place from where he fell is believed to be the center of the Big Dipper.

Other landmarks in the Black Hills were formed when all the animals ran a race to determine whether or not "two-leggeds" (humans) were going to remain on this earth. Human beings had erred in many ways, so many of the animals sought to cleanse the earth. Other animals, however, like the Magpie, wanted the two-leggeds to continue living with them on the earth. As the animals thundered over the ground, the force of their hooves and paws made rocks rise and protrude the earth, thereby forming the Black Hills. Toward the end of the race, the Magpie, refreshed from riding on the backs of the other animals as they ran, flew across the finish line first. Since the Magpie won the race, the two-leggeds were allowed to continue living on this earth. This story reinforces the Sioux belief that they have existed as long as the Black Hills.

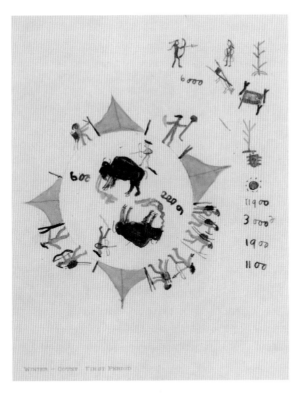

Winter Counts are hide pictographs used to record history.

The sacred Black Hills were promised to the Sioux forever but then taken away when gold was found there.

The Black Hills' Harney Peak, named for an American explorer, is called Hinhan Kaga Paha (Owl Maker Hill) by the Oceti Sakowin (the Sioux). This formation also has its story.

Long ago, a band of Sioux was camped near the rock formation that is today called Harney Peak. During the night, a little girl was fretful and cried. Her mother tried to comfort her—but to no avail. Frustrated, the mother threatened that if the little girl didn't stop crying, she would put her outside. The little girl continued crying—and she was placed outside.

When the mother no longer heard crying, she went outside to get the little girl—but the child had disappeared. The mother and those with her frantically searched for the little girl, but she was nowhere to be found. A large bird had swooped down and taken her to the top of the mountain and killed her.

In each of the six days that followed, this same large bird came to the camp and took a girl child. Desperate, the people prayed to Fallen Star . . . and he finally came to their rescue. He killed the large bird and took the spirits of the seven little girls up to the sky. They have remained in the sky ever since as the Pleiades constellation, which the Sioux call the Wicincala Sakowin (Seven Little Girls).

Creation stories like these were told during the winter when the nights were long. They were told, remembered, and retold, passing from generation to generation.

Another type of tale was the Wicowoyake (historical stories), which were told for informational purposes. Like the creation stories, these historical tales were usually kept for the long winter hours, when they would be recounted by the keeper of the oral traditions. One such story is the coming of the Ptesan Win (White Buffalo Calf Woman) in 1540.

Two young men were out scouting when they saw something in the distance. As they approached, they saw that it was a beautiful young woman. One man knew that this was a sacred woman and looked upon her with respect, but the other man reached out for her with greedy hands. A cloud enveloped him, and when it cleared, his bones lay bare on the earth.

The young woman asked the remaining young man to take a message back to his people. She told him what preparations the people must make for her visit. He carried her instructions to his camp, and they immediately prepared for her arrival. On the designated day, she walked toward the camp with a bundle in her arms, singing a song as she came among them.

The Creator had seen how the people were living with hardship in this world, so he had sent her to help them. She gave advice to the leaders, and to the men, women, and children on how they were to conduct themselves with respect and humility, and how they were to live in harmony with all living things. Opening her bundle, she brought out a pipe and gave the people instructions on how to use it.

She told the people everything about the seven sacred ceremonies, and then she rose, walked clockwise within a circle, and left. In the distance, the people saw her roll over four times; when she stood, she had become a white buffalo. Then she disappeared over the horizon.

In the years following her appearance, specially chosen people were

Another View of Mount Rushmore

Gazing out across our sacred Black Hills are the faces of Presidents Washington, Jefferson, Roosevelt, and Lincoln—Mount Rushmore, a so-called "shrine" to democracy. But how can a shrine celebrating democracy be carved into land that . . . was illegally seized and occupied?

George Washington was responsible for the annihilation of tens of thousands of sovereign tribal members.

Thomas Jefferson, a prolific slave owner, set westward expansion in motion and made Manifest Destiny and the genocide of Native people west of the Mississippi a reality.

Teddy Roosevelt was responsible for some of the greatest acts of theft from sovereign Indian Nations in history.

Abraham Lincoln was an "Indian Fighter."

For us, these individuals are far from shining beacons of democracy.

From www.lakotaoyate.com, a Web site initiated by a group of traditionalists based on the Pine Ridge Reservation who have united in an attempt to defend and preserve Lakota culture from exploitation.

given dreams and visions on how the seven sacred ceremonies were to be performed. The seven sacred ceremonies were:

- Inipi (sweat lodge)
- Hanbleceya (vision quest)
- Hunka (making of relatives)
- Wiwanyang Wacipi (Sun Dance)
- Isnati Awicalowanpi (making a buffalo woman)
- Tapa Wankayeyapi (tossing of the ball)
- Nagi Gluhapi (keeping of the Spirit)

All seven sacred ceremonies were equally important and were connected together, so if a person performed them sincerely, the practice would lead to a well-balanced, self-fulfilled individual.

Since the 1970s, with the passage of the Indian Religious Freedom Act, there has been a resurgence of young people who are seeking to reclaim the sacred ceremonies that were banned by the U.S. government in the early 1900s. These young people seek the knowledge and understanding that their forefathers were forbidden.

This memorial at Wounded Knee marks the spot where on December 29, 1890, troops of the Seventh Calvary massacred a gathering of Lakota Indians.

Chapter 2

History

A couple of days before December 29, 1890, all Indian scouts across the reservation were summoned to report to the Indian Agency. The scouts gathered in Pine Ridge and anxiously awaited further orders. They were uneasy because they knew Chief Big Foot and his band of Mniconjou were traveling to the Pine Ridge Agency to "surrender." The U.S. Seventh Cavalry was positioned in Wounded Knee waiting to escort Chief Big Foot to the agency. The Indian scouts waited as well.

Wounded Knee is located less than twenty miles as the crow flies northeast of Pine Ridge. On that calm day in 1890, those who stood waiting for the chief heard cannons exploding and gunshots echoing in the distance. The Indian scouts were kept back in Pine Ridge—and then a blizzard descended on the whole area. After the blizzard had passed, the scouts were ordered to Wounded Knee. There they found the massacred remains of Chief Big Foot and his people. The Indian scouts' duty was to dig a mass grave, collect the bodies, and deposit them into the ground.

The portable tepee provided warm and efficient shelter for the traveling bands of Oceti Sakowin after they acquired horses and before they were forced onto reservations.

As Samuel Rock, one of many Indian scouts employed on the reservation, was dutifully performing his task, he came across his father's body among the dead. Stricken with grief and shock, he requested that his father, Ghost Horse, be taken to Porcupine seven miles to the north for a proper burial. His request was denied by the Indian Agency. Numb and disbelieving, he had to place his father's body into the mass grave with all the other massacre victims. This is perhaps one of the saddest stories in Sioux history—but it connects the realities of the past with the struggles of contemporary Sioux societies.

Before European contact, the Sioux Nation consisted of seven major divisions, which called themselves the Oceti Sakowin—the Seven Council Fires.

The Dakota, or the *Mdewakantonwan* (People of Spirit Lake), dwelled to the east and northeast of the lakes region within the vast territory that the Oceti Sakowin commanded. The majority of the Dakota economy centered on fishing and the harvesting of wild rice and herbs. The Dakota were known and recognized as the "People of the Herbs." They included the following groups:

- the Wahpekute (Shooters Among the Leaves)
- the Wahpetonwan (Dwellers Among the Leaves)
- the Sisitonwan (People of the Swamp).

To the southwest of the Dakota were the Nakota. They included:

- the Ihanktonwan (Campers at the End)
- the Ihanktonwanna (Little Campers at the End)

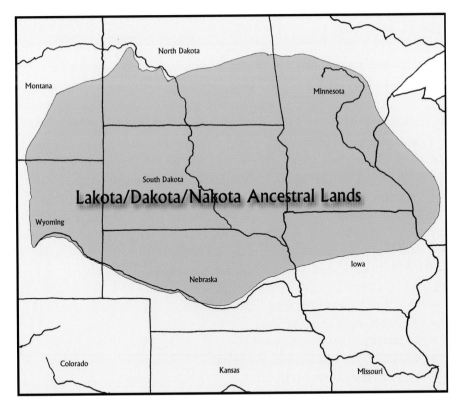

Map of Sioux ancestral lands.

The Badlands of South Dakota were traditionally home to the Lakota bands. Today, the southern half of Badlands National Park is located on the Pine Ridge Lakota Nation.

- the Assiniboine (Cook with Stones). This group was not one of the original divisions of the Sioux, but the band became associated with the Nakota divisions in the pre-reservation era.

The Nakota resided to the southeast and south within the Oceti Sakowin territory. Their economy centered on pipestone quarrying, and they were known and recognized as the caretakers and protectors of the quarries.

The Lakota consisted of seven smaller subdivisions or bands:

- the Sichangu (Burnt Thighs)
- the Oohenunpa (Two Kettles)
- the Itazipacola (Without Bows)
- the Mniconjou (Planters by the Water)
- the Sihasapa (Black Feet)
- the Hunkpapa (End of the Horn or Entrance)
- the Oglala (Scatter Their Own)

The Lakota were known as the "People of the Prairie" and the *Pte Oyate* (Buffalo People). They resided on the Great Plains region to the west, northwest, and the southwest of the main Oceti Sakowin territory. Their economy depended on the buffalo and the wild fruits and vegetables of the plains. They were also known and recognized as the caretakers and protectors of the Black Hills, which they and the Oceti Sakowin referred to as *He Sapa*.

The Sioux depended on each other for survival. How they traded with one another reflected where they lived and what they could provide other groups. Whether they were twenty miles apart or four hundred, the various groups communicated constantly with one another.

Their lifestyles were ideally suited to their climate and could be adjusted to sudden shifts in conditions. Such an adjustment occurred annually at the time of the religious and social gathering, when the entire nation came together. This was a time for family socializing and for the various leaders to meet for major decision making.

The Sioux contend that they have always lived in the northern Great Plains area. If a migration occurred, they say, it was outward from the

Eyewitness to a Massacre

There was a woman with an infant in her arms who was killed as she almost touched the flag of truce, and the women and children of course were strewn all along the circular village until they were dispatched. Right near the flag of truce a mother was shot down with her infant; the child not knowing that its mother was dead was still nursing, and that especially was a very sad sight. The women as they were fleeing with their babes were killed together, shot right through, and the women who were very heavy with child were also killed. All the Indians fled in these three directions, and after most all of them had been killed a cry was made that all those who were not killed should come forth and they would be safe. Little boys who were not wounded came out of their places of refuge, and as soon as they came in sight a number of soldiers surrounded them and butchered them there.

—American Horse of the Oglala Sioux, 1891

In 1903, Joseph Horn Cloud, along with friends and family members, had this monument set at the site of the mass grave at Wounded Knee. The inscription reads in part: "Big Foot was a great Chief of the Sioux Indians. He often said, 'I will stand in peace till my last day comes.' He did many good and brave deeds for the white man and the red man. Many innocent women and children who knew no wrong died here."

Black Hills into the outlying regions. Because the Black Hills are the traditional birthplace of the Sioux Nation, the Black Hills have a strong religious significance for the Oceti Sakowin, particularly the Lakota.

The entire Black Hills region has always been known to the Sioux as "the heart of everything that is," because within the Black Hills lie the people's psychological and physical healing elements. Religious ceremonies were traditionally conducted at various sites in the hills, beginning in the spring and continuing throughout the summer in accordance with the movement of the constellations. The Oceti Sakowin as a whole never resided in the Black Hills for long periods of time (nor do most North Americans live in their churches), but the Sioux always returned annually for the religious and social gathering.

Throughout the rest of the year, the Oceti Sakowin lived in their respective regions. They never lived in one large encampment, but rather in smaller groups called *tiospaye*, which consisted of immediate family members, extended family, and others who chose to live with that particular tiospaye. Many tiospaye were within any given division of the Oceti Sakowin. Although these were located near enough to each other so that they were never isolated, they maintained the privacy and space needed for comfortable living. Their life may not have been perfect, but it was peaceful.

Everything changed when the newcomers from abroad arrived in their land. The first encounter—with the Spanish—took place in the Rocky Mountains. From the Spanish, the Sioux acquired horses. Because of the horse's outstanding ability to do many things, the Sioux called it *sun-kawakan*, "sacred-holy dog." The horse was also considered sacred or holy

When Edward Curtis took this picture in 1907, it had been decades since the Lakota were forced to live on reservations. The title of the picture, Oglala War Party, *was intended to help sell the picture to an American public enamored by Wild West war stories.*

Oglala Lakota Crazy Horse was born on Rapid Creek around 1845. While at Fort Robinson, Nebraska, under a flag of truce, he was stabbed in the back by an American soldier and died September 6, 1877. He defended his people and their way of life with great courage and honor. Boston-born sculptor Korczak Ziolkowski began working in 1939 on behalf of the Sioux people to carve a monument to Crazy Horse in the Black Hills.

because its arrival had been revealed to the people through prophecy. Their encounter with the Spanish thus allowed the Oceti Sakowin to make positive changes within their culture.

The second encounter occurred with French traders and trappers at the place where the Mississippi and Missouri Rivers meet. The two cultures got along well at first, and when the trade moved up the Missouri River, the strong alliance continued. Marriages between the French traders and Oceti Sakowin women became commonplace and acceptable. Guns were introduced, as well as household wares, a development that eventually resulted in the Sioux becoming less dependent on the buffalo. Because the traders often lived and interacted within the bands and learned the language, they and their offspring later served as interpreters. Many of the descendents of these traders and Oceti Sakowin women continue to live in Sioux communities as tribal members.

For a time, the Oceti Sakowin bands struggled for control and management of their traditional government system and territory. The Euro-American westward expansion continued, however, and the Oceti Sakowin gradually lost control over their once vast territory.

The United States seized land through treaties. These documents set boundaries for tribes and limited the Sioux's natural lifestyle and freedom. The first major treaty for the Oceti Sakowin was the 1851 Fort Laramie Treaty, which called for peace among the northern tribes, the establishment of roads and military posts, protection for Indians, and the establishment of boundaries.

The second major treaty was the 1868 Fort Laramie Treaty. Its terms reduced the boundaries set in the 1851 treaty to the western half of present-day South Dakota, an area to be called the Great Sioux Reservation. It also called for the Sioux to change their culture and become like non-Indians through the acceptance of Christianity and educational programs that would encourage *assimilation*.

The U.S. government ceased treaty making in 1871, but when gold was discovered within the boundaries of the Great Sioux Reservation in the Black Hills, federal authorities attempted to negotiate with the Oceti

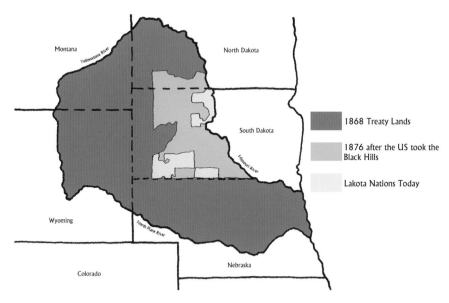

Map of shrinking Lakota lands.

Sakowin for the sale of the Black Hills region. Unable to reach a negotiated agreement, the government, meeting with a group of Sioux who did not represent the majority of the Oceti Sakowin, pushed through a document that removed the Black Hills region from the Great Sioux Reservation. The Oceti Sakowin still dispute this violation. They have refused to accept any monetary payment for the Black Hills lands that were taken from them.

The establishment of settled reservations in the 1880s was marred by fear and distrust of the U.S. government. A land "agreement," the Dawes Allotment Act of 1889, reduced the land base of the Great Sioux Reservation dramatically. The new policy of allotment enrolled tribal heads of household, their spouses, and children, and then assigned them to individual homesteads. Once all enrolled tribal members received their allotments, the surplus lands were opened to *homesteaders*, further reducing the size of Indian lands.

The 1990 U.S. Census indicated that there are 103,255 enrolled members of the Sioux. They reside on reservations in South Dakota, North

Pine Ridge Reservation in South Dakota is the second largest North American Indian reservation and is home to the Oglala Lakota. The reservation today is just a tiny portion of lands originally promised to the Sioux by the U.S. government.

This is how Crazy Horse memorial looked in 2002. Crazy Horse's pointing finger reminds viewers of a famous quote. When asked, "Where are your lands now?" Crazy Horse pointed and said, "My lands are where my dead lie buried."

Dakota, Minnesota, Nebraska, and Montana. The census figure does not include the Sioux who reside in Canada or non-enrolled tribal members.

The descendents of the original Oceti Sakowin have a long history. Despite years of conflict with the U.S. government, their heritage ties them as firmly as ever to the Black Hills.

Chief Red Cloud was a great Oglala Lakota leader of the nineteenth century.

Chapter 3

Current Government

Tribal *primary election* day on the Pine Ridge Indian Reservation, October 8, 2002, was marked with turmoil, although many tribal members were unaware of this strife. The candidates for tribal president were *incumbent* president John Yellow Bird Steele, incumbent vice president Theresa Two Bulls, *activist* Russell Means, past vice president Mel Lone Hill, and Denver American Horse. There was excitement as the votes were tallied throughout the evening hours and announced over KILI radio station, owned by the Oglala people. According to the unofficial results, Russell Means won the primary election by several hundred votes over the incumbent president.

The top two candidates were to appear on the ballot for the general election on November 5, 2002. Some members of the tribe were not happy about the results of the primary election, however, and they launched a *smear campaign* against Russell Means. Disgruntled tribal members also brought allegations of *ballot box tampering* against the election board. Some board members were fired and replaced with new members.

A Russell Means campaign sign on the Pine Ridge Reservation recalls the controversial tribal election of 2002.

A few days before the November election, a decision was made by the tribal council to redo the primary election on November 5, 2002, and hold the general election on November 19, 2002. Angry voters reluctantly went back to the polls on November 5, but the outcome of that election was not much different from the one in October. Russell Means and John Yellow Bird Steele were still the top two candidates. On November 19, 2002, John Yellow Bird Steele was reelected tribal president.

The current tribal government came into existence with the Indian Reorganization Act of 1934 (IRA), which called for a *constitution* and government system patterned after the U.S. Constitution and the federal government. The Oglala Sioux Tribe voted to accept the IRA on December 14, 1935, and they seated their first tribal council on April 4, 1936. This act symbolized the end of traditional government, since the Bureau of Indian Affairs agent overruled the traditional leadership and appointed "progressives" to enforce laws on the reservation. Other Sioux tribes eventually adopted the IRA government and currently operate under that system.

The Sioux people continue to struggle with the IRA, however. This act conflicts with the traditional government system by taking the power from the people, who had traditionally operated with natural laws from pre-reservation days. According to these unwritten laws, *Itancan* (leaders) were people who displayed wisdom, courage, generosity, honesty, respect, humility, and who always carried the people in their heart. The people were the ones who made the Itancan by following him as long as he was effective. If the people became displeased with their Itancan, they were free to leave and join another tiospaye that suited their needs. The Itancan position was not hereditary. Just because an Itancan had a son didn't mean his position would automatically be passed on to the next generation. If the son displayed the qualities and earned the respect of the people, he also had a chance to be elevated to the position of Itancan. Under this system, there was no need for the people to ever express their displeasure by revolting and attempting to overthrow the Itancan.

Fluidity was a trademark of this traditional government. Some groups dissolved because of poor leadership, while new ones came into existence, and others flourished as they gained members. This way of doing things was strange to Europeans; many historians who attempted to document and write a history of the pre-reservation Oceti Sakowin have misconstrued some of their findings. Today's government is far different from the traditional one. Their growing displeasure over the current tribal government has prompted some tribal members to take action to change the system—but this has proven to be a slow process.

Tribal government offices at Pine Ridge Reservation, South Dakota.

This is the Bureau of Indian Affairs office in Pine Ridge Reservation, South Dakota. The BIA remains an important part of Native American communities today, although its policies have often been criticized.

There are currently nine districts on the Pine Ridge Reservation:

- Eagle Nest
- Pass Creek
- Lacreek
- Wakpamni
- Porcupine
- Wounded Knee
- Oglala
- Kyle
- Pine Ridge Village

All have elected officials who serve the people within that district. Each district elects representatives according to their own district population (one to two representatives, with the exception of Pine Ridge Village who has three), for a total of eighteen members who serve on the tribal council. Along with the Executive Committee—comprised of the president, vice president, secretary, treasurer, and a fifth member—they serve as the governing body for the entire reservation population.

Tribal council members are full-time employees who meet at least once a month for several days at a time; special meetings are held when required. The rest of their time is spent in their respective district or meeting with their chosen committee at the Tribal Headquarters. They are required to serve on a minimum of two of the following established committees: education, land, health and human services, economic development, or finance. Each committee addresses issues related to that particular area through discussion, presentation, and finally recommendation to the full council.

In the beginning of the IRA government, people didn't talk much about women's rights. Only the male population participated in the government as voting members, while the women attended as nonvoting members. Eventually, twenty to thirty years after the system began, women were included and elected to serve as representatives. So far, however, no female has ever served as tribal president of the Oglala Sioux Tribe. The tribe did, however, elect their first female vice president, Theresa Two Bulls, who served from 2000 to 2002; she was unsuccessful in her bid for the tribal presidency in 2002. The election of 2002 seated nine female representatives on the tribal council, half of the council. One other member of the Oceti Sakowin, the Flandreau Santee Sioux Tribe, overcame the gender barrier (at least temporarily) when they elected their first female tribal president, Agnes Ross.

In the pre-reservation period, gender was never an issue because each sex lived according to prescribed male and female roles. Survival required that everyone behave in a manner that would protect, clothe, and feed the tribe at all times. Male and female roles complemented one another, and the sexes lived as equals. Men endangered their lives to protect the camps and hunt for food—and women processed the game, gathered wild vegetables and berries, raised the children, made the clothing, and basically did everything else it took to make a home. European explorers and traders were comfortable with these traditional roles, but most of them failed to notice that among the Oceti Sakowin, the woman also owned everything and had the right to make decisions regarding her own welfare. She had the right to divorce her husband, if she chose, without losing her dignity.

This woman at the National Powwow in Washington, DC, in December of 2002 displays the dignity of her Plains Indian heritage. Equality between the sexes, as well as the traditional government system, was temporarily lost during the change to reservation life and the process of Indian culture being put down by the U.S. government.

Respected, mature women were sometimes invited to address council gatherings.

The traditional system of government and equality between the sexes were lost temporarily during the change to reservation life; this process meant that Indian culture was often devalued. Women were not allowed to participate in politics, and many older traditional "chiefs" (a term used by the U.S. government agent) were removed by the government and replaced by younger "progressive" men. The Indian Agent appointed these young men to be chief in an effort to make the Indians live more like whites—completely disregarding the fact that these people already had their own legitimate form of government.

In a recent college American history class, a professor made a comment while discussing **Manifest Destiny** and westward expansion: "The tribes had to be conquered because they had no form of government." Native people did, however, have their own government, even if it was unwritten. The many tribes in North America could not have coexisted side by side for centuries before European contact without some sort of system to maintain order. The lack of knowledge, sensitivity, and openness demonstrated by this professor is an example of the attitudes that have created barriers between the Indian and European cultures.

This building is headquarters for Wakpami Law Enforcement Services of the Oglala Lakota on Pine Ridge Reservation, South Dakota. The Oglala Sioux Tribal Police is overseen by the elected tribal Public Safety Commission.

Lady of Sorrows Catholic Church in Kyle is one of the Christian churches on Pine Ridge Reservation today.

Chapter 4

Today's Religion

In the early twentieth century, a Dakota *Presbyterian* minister, Samuel K. Weston, his wife Martha Redwing, and their four young children made their way westward from Flandreau, South Dakota. Their destination was the Pine Ridge Indian Reservation located in the remote southwestern part of South Dakota. They came to share Christian beliefs with the Lakota people, their distant relatives. Reverend and Mrs. Weston's younger children would be born on the Pine Ridge Reservation, and there the family would soon experience a tremendous change in their lifestyle. As Weston traveled toward Pine Ridge, the Minnesota Uprising of 1862 must have been still fresh in his memory.

On August 15, 1862, Sioux Chief Little Crow had gone to the Indian Agency to ask government agent Thomas J. Galbraith to distribute provisions to his hungry people. "We have no food, but here are these stores filled with food," he yelled at Galbraith.

Holy Rosary Catholic Mission on Pine Ridge Oglala Lakota Reservation in South Dakota.

"So far as I'm concerned, if they are hungry, let them eat grass or their own **dung**," was the reply.

Many of the Sioux had finally had enough of the white man. They decided that with the United States engaged in the Civil War, the time had come to reclaim their land. Little Crow knew they had little chance of defeating the U.S. army, but he told his braves, "Little Crow is not a coward; he will die with you!"

By the end of the uprising, two thousand Indians were captured and tried, and a military board sentenced 303 to be hanged. President Abraham Lincoln reviewed the list and trimmed it to 38. The United States' largest public mass execution was held December 26, 1862, when the 38 Indians were hanged. Weston and his family had witnessed the terrible fate of those who had resisted the American government.

As Weston and his family traveled by wagon, he knew that life as he once knew it would never be the same. They crossed the Missouri River on a ferry, knowing they would never return as permanent residents to live among their own people.

In accordance with the 1868 Fort Laramie Treaty, all Indians had to relocate within the boundaries of the established reservations. As part of the assimilation process of the treaty, churches and schools were to be built to Christianize and educate Indian children and their families. Weston's mission was to assist in the Christianization of the Lakota people. The U.S government had banned native religious practices; Weston knew that he would be challenged by the people's unrest and fear.

His first assignment was in the community of Porcupine, where a church had been built on donated land from tribal member, Amos Lone Hill. Samuel later served Presbyterian churches in Oglala and Allen. His four youngest children married Oglala tribal members. His acceptance into these communities was the result of the common bond of language and culture; he lived and talked like an Indian. Although he worked diligently

This is a picture of a Cheyenne Sun Dance lodge taken by Edward Curtis early in the twentieth century. For most of the last century, the U.S. government outlawed this vitally important part of Plains Indian spiritual practice. It was only recently reintroduced, and Native spiritual leaders are careful to protect it against imitation or suppression by outsiders.

The Sweat Lodge

The Sweat Ceremony is one way traditional North American Indians communicate with God. Prayers in the sweat lodge may be for loved ones, for those who are ill, or for power to face a challenge. Some people partake in sweat lodge ceremonies several times a year; some do daily.

A dome-shaped framework is made from willow saplings. This is covered with blankets or skins. A spiritual leader blesses it. Water is poured over heated rocks, releasing hot steam into the lodge, and the doorway is covered by a flap. Temperatures inside rise to over 200 degrees Fahrenheit. Spoken prayers are combined with prayers through the use of cedar bark, sage, or sweet grass incense. The sweat also has physical value, since it removes toxins from the body.

among the people with his Bible in hand, he was known to also pray while he smoked his Native pipe in the evenings.

In 1979, however, Weston's granddaughter severely reprimanded her children for attending traditional Lakota ceremonies; she claimed that these ceremonies were evil. This attitude of cultural shame had been instilled in a couple of generations of children who attended the mission boarding schools and the government boarding schools in the early 1900s, and the same attitude continued through the 1960s. Unaffected by the mother's fears, Weston's great grandchildren continued to attend traditional religious practices, explaining that these beautiful and meaningful spiritual experiences explained existence in this world. Eventually, Weston's granddaughter participated and learned that she could worship God here as well as in a Christian service; everyone prayed to the same Creator.

The *Protestants* produced a number of Indian ministers besides Samuel Weston. Episcopalian ministers from other reservations included Vine Deloria and Chris Whipple, who also served churches on the Pine Ridge Reservation during the same period as Weston. These ministers lived among

This artist's rendition of Sitting Bull uses Native religious symbolism. Around the figure's head, in place of a halo, is a medicine wheel, a symbol of life's never-ending cycle. The cycle begins with birth, moves through maturity to old age and death, and comes back to rebirth (either here or in the spirit world). The four bars that divide the wheel represent the four directions (north, south, east, west) and everything that dwells in those areas; the west represents danger and death, the north life, the east knowledge, and the south quiet. The buffalo skull is a symbol of the Great Spirit's wisdom and generosity, since the buffalo gave the Sioux people food, clothing, tools, medicine, and shelter. The eagle feather is a sacred symbol, because the eagle flies the highest of all birds and thus is able to carry prayers to the Great Spirit. The red border on Sitting Bull's robe stands for the earth and for the blood that was shed for his people.

Stained glass windows in the Holy Rosary Catholic Mission include traditional Lakota designs.

Food for Thought

Some decades ago I attended a burial in a Christian cemetery at Mission, South Dakota. After the body was in the grave and the several mourners were standing at the grave, an old woman stepped forward and put an orange on the grave. The Episcopal priest who had conducted the service rushed over and took the orange away, saying, "When do you think the departed will come and eat this orange?" One of the Sioux men standing there said, "When the Soul comes to smell the flowers." No one said anything after that!

—Vine Deloria, Jr., Hunkpapa Lakota author

the people and spoke the same language; as a result, they established good relationships.

The Catholic Church, meanwhile, established missions that served two purposes: building churches to convert tribal members and establishing boarding schools to educate the young. Historically, the most notable Lakota Catholic individual was Black Elk. He attempted to understand Christianity (after he was forced to do so) and was baptized Nicholas Black Elk on December 6, 1904, at the Holy Rosary Mission near present-day Pine Ridge, South Dakota.

Although the role of faithful Catholic was forced on him, he played it well to satisfy his oppressors. Black Elk's Lakota spirituality, however, also remained strong throughout his life. He was part of the *underground* traditional religious movement, which began shortly after the U.S. government banned native religious practices. These underground activities became a vital part of Black Elk's life—as did his visible life as a faithful Catholic. He mastered both, but he feared that U.S. policies would overcome the Lakota Nation and destroy his people's identity.

Many of the Lakota traditional healers and holy men and women of that time shared Black Elk's philosophy. Some chose to record—through non-Indian writers—the Lakota's sacred knowledge and information in the

"Hear me, four quarters of the world—a relative I am! Give me the strength to walk the soft earth, a relative to all that is! Give me the eyes to see and the strength to understand, that I may be like you. With your power only can I face the winds."
—Black Elk (1863–1950), Oglala Sioux holy man

hope of preserving oral traditions for the future generations of the Lakota people.

Black Elk also committed himself to the task of recording his sacred knowledge and information. During the summer of 1930, he dictated his life story to John Neihardt, and the resulting book, *Black Elk Speaks*, appeared in 1932. Reprinted many times, the book was widely circulated and read by the general public.

Many Sioux during this time feared that their culture would cease to exist. George Sword and others like him followed Black Elk's example and shared sacred information with James Walker, a physician who was entrusted to publish their words after they had died. The book was titled *Lakota Belief and Ritual*.

When Sioux like Black Elk went public with their stories, they offered not only their own people but all humankind an understanding of their

Real Peace

The First Peace, which is the most important, is that which comes within the Souls of men when they realize their relationship, their oneness, with the Universe and all its Powers, and when they realize that at the center of the Universe dwells Wakan Tanka, and that this center is really everywhere, it is within each of us. This is the real Peace, and the others are but reflections of this. The Second Peace is that which is between two individuals, and the third is that which is made between two nations. But above all you should understand that there can never be Peace between nations until there is first known that True Peace which, as I have often said, is within the Souls of men.

—Black Elk

people's history and a sense of hope for the future. Black Elk's vision eventually became a message to the entire Oceti Sakowin. It was a warning that if they accepted all the ways of the non-Native people around them, they would lose their rich traditions and cease to exist as a unique nation. This message was evident in his final words: "There is no center any longer, and the sacred tree is dead."

The passage of the Indian Religious Freedom Act in 1978 lifted the fear of federal prosecution and allowed the Lakota Nation free expression and open practice of its centuries-old religion. The combination of this legislation and the popularity of Black Elk's teachings created a new beginning for Lakota spirituality. This new movement has resulted in smaller membership in Christian services across the reservations. In an attempt to hold onto members, some Christian churches have incorporated minimal Sioux traditions, but the move toward true traditional spirituality has continued to grow, particularly among the younger generation.

Today, young and old are free to express their spirituality in whatever manner they choose. They may choose to go into the Inipi (sweat lodge) to pray, or they may attend one of the Christian churches, or they may do both. A number of different faiths are present on the reservations today: Mormon, Jehovah's Witness, the Native American Church, Catholic, Episcopal, Presbyterian, Baptist, and many other Christian denominations. Most children are being raised with traditional spiritual practices in the home, while the churches serve as places for social gatherings.

The Sioux find it difficult to separate religion from the rest of life. For the Oceti Sakowin, spirituality was part of everything a person did; it was never separated from daily life, never shut up inside a building where people gathered to pray for an hour or two once a week. The Oceti Sakowin found their "church" wherever they wanted it to be—for it was within their heart. They prayed when they awoke, before they went to sleep, before and after the hunt, before going to war and after returning, before and after meetings. . . . Each event in life was an occasion for prayer.

Religious rituals were performed during the ceremonies. The Inipi (sweat lodge), Hanbleceya (vision quest), Wiwang Wacipi (Sun Dance), Hunka (making of relatives), Isnati Awicalowanpi (making a Buffalo Woman), Tapa Wankayeyapi (tossing the ball), and the Nagi Gluhapi (keeping the Spirit) were all rituals that led to an understanding of one's place in this world. All these ceremonies were connected, and a young person learned them as he or she traveled through life.

This lifelong process began at the Hunka Ceremony, when a child received a name bestowed by the Creator. This name affirmed each child's unique identity. Relatives or groups of people could also be adopted through this ceremony.

Many families today have gone back to practicing these ceremonies. Since the Indian Religious Freedom Act of 1978, all seven ceremonies have been back in practice to some extent, some more than others. The Inipi (sweat lodge) is practiced year round; the Hanbleceya (vision quest) is done primarily in the spring; the Wiwanyang Wacipi (Sun Dance) is done after the summer *solstice* and into August; the Hunka (making of relatives) is done during social gatherings in the summer months; and the other three are done when necessary and as requested by individual families.

After a century of attempted annihilation of their traditional religious practices, the spirituality of today's Oceti Sakowin has been revived and is becoming stronger. More and more people are depending on traditional ways to achieve happiness and live in balance with themselves and the world. However, this does not mean that all Sioux have given up Christianity in favor of the traditional practices. Many still consider themselves Christians, but feel that traditional practices are compatible with their Christian beliefs.

Today the Sioux have their own schools.

Chapter 5

Social Structures Today

Beginning in 1879 and continuing through the 1920s, reservation children were taken from their parents and sent to boarding schools in Carlisle, Pennsylvania; Hampton, Virginia; and Genoa, Nebraska, in an effort to "Americanize" them. Luthor Standing Bear described his experience of riding the train with other children for days, not knowing where they were going. Many of these children never returned home and were buried in distant school cemeteries.

Upon arrival at the Carlisle Indian School, the children's clothing was replaced by school uniforms, their hair was cut, and they were forced to speak the foreign language of English. The teacher wrote words on the blackboard, and each child took a turn hitting one of the words with the stick. Luthor Standing Bear said it was like counting coup. (Indian warriors

After high school completion, the majority of Indian students who went to college in the 1950s and 1960s, dropped out. Some Lakota visionaries chartered Oglala Lakota College in 1971. It has been highly successful.

"counted coup" by touching their enemy with a stick.) This was how he chose the name of Luthor. One frustrated little boy had to hit the blackboard many times before the teacher finally gave the boy a name; the names he was choosing were female names.

Nearly one hundred years later, the Indian Self-Determination and Education Assistance Act of 1975 granted tribes the right to contract the operations of Bureau of Indian Affairs programs. On the Pine Ridge Reservation, community people took immediate advantage of this opportunity to gain control of their children's education. Loneman School (kindergarten through eighth grade) in Oglala, Little Wound School (kindergarten through twelfth grade) in Kyle, Crazy Horse School (kindergarten through twelfth grade) in Wanblee, Porcupine School (kindergarten through eighth grade) in Porcupine, Wounded Knee District School (kindergarten through eighth grade) in Manderson, and American Horse School (kindergarten through eighth grade) in Allen are all schools operated by the tribe. Locally elected tribal members serve on these school boards and have formed the Oglala Nation Education Coalition (ONEC), comprised of all the reservation schools boards.

There are other schools on the Pine Ridge Reservation as well: the private Catholic parochial schools of Red Cloud Indian School near Pine Ridge (formerly Holy Rosary Mission) and Our Lady of Lourdes in Porcupine; the Shannon County Schools at Wolf Creek, Batesland, Rockyford, and Red Shirt; and the only school still operated by the Bureau of Indian Affairs in Pine Ridge.

Indian children no longer attend boarding schools, unless the parents choose to send them to one of the remaining boarding schools still in operation. The Bureau of Indian Affairs continues to operate the boarding schools in Pine Ridge and Flandreau, South Dakota. Most Sioux children, however, attend one of the many schools on the reservation.

The majority of Indian students who went on to college in the 1950s and 1960s dropped out and returned to the reservations. Hoping to help more Sioux young people get a college education, some Lakota visionaries decided to take action and chartered Oglala Lakota College in 1971. The tribal college has provided higher education and granted degrees to many tribal members, as well as nontribal members. It is a fully *accredited* institution that offers two- and four-year degrees in business, education, Lakota studies, agriculture and natural resources, human services, humanities, nursing, math, science, and technology; and master's degrees in education and Lakota leadership and management. The college is unique because its *curriculum* incorporates the Lakota perspective into the learning process. The college currently averages 1,300 to 1,400 students per semester.

There are other tribal colleges that also offer this unique educational opportunity: Sinte Gleska University on the Rosebud Reservation, Sitting Bull College on the Standing Rock Reservation, Si Tanka-Huron on the Cheyenne River Reservation, and Sisseton-Wahpeton Community College on the Sisseton Reservation, all serving their respective reservation communities. All the tribal colleges are a part of the American Indian Higher Education Consortium (AIHEC), which is comprised of all tribal colleges in the United States.

Indian children no longer attend boarding schools, unless the parents choose to send them to one of the remaining boarding schools still in operation. Most Indian children attend one of the many schools on the reservation.

Little Wound School, in Kyle, on the Pine Ridge Reservation, provides education, including Lakota culture and bilingual education, at elementary and high school levels.

The federal government still operates health care facilities on most of the Sioux reservations, with some services contracted out to larger off-reservation facilities. The major health facility on the Pine Ridge Reservation is located in the village of Pine Ridge, but some of the outlying districts, such as Manderson, Porcupine, Kyle, and Wanblee, have local clinics. The majority of the doctors and dentists who provide services are still non-Indian, but the nursing and support staff are comprised of tribal members.

Although health care facilities are available, some tribal members have opted to return to traditional health and healing practices. Since the ban was lifted in 1978, some non-Indian health care professionals have worked with traditional *medicine men* and healers. The times have changed. In the past, non-Indians looked down on traditional ways and tried to do away with them. Now there is a growing attitude of mutual understanding and respect.

Social service agencies on the reservations are primarily operated by the state with little or no input from tribal members. The majority of social workers are non-Indians who commute from surrounding off-reservation towns. Because high unemployment on the reservation is still an issue, many Sioux families depend on state assistance. Elderly people and others requiring nursing home assistance are often placed in nursing homes off the reservation. State rules have not allowed nursing homes to be built on the reservation.

The Sioux have their own law and order agencies. The Oglala Sioux Tribal Council and its judiciary committee oversee the Oglala Sioux Tribal Court, while the Oglala Sioux Tribal Police is supervised by the elected Public Safety Commission. The two courthouses and jails are located in Pine Ridge and Kyle. A chief judge, associate judges, and prosecutors are employed within this system. Each district has police officers hired and appointed by the Public Safety Commission to maintain order.

The U.S. military has attracted many young Oceti Sakowin men and women into its services. This began with World War I—even before they were declared citizens of the United States. (All American Indians became U.S. citizens in 1924.) Today it isn't unusual to find at least two members of each household who served or are currently serving in the U.S. military. Some people have attributed this high rate of service to the fact that traditional duties included protection of one's territory through warfare. Respect and honor came to those who courageously defended their people and territory. With the establishment of the reservations, service in the military also became a way to display bravery.

The Wacipi (powwows) are social gatherings where Native people come together to dance and conduct some of their ceremonies. They are a time to visit old friends and make new ones. Powwows were held primarily outdoors during the summer months, but today, some powwows are held indoors

The SuAnne Big Crow Boys & Girls Club was originally opened in 1992—the first Boys & Girls Club established on Native American lands. Named for SuAnne Big Crow, a young Lakota heroine who was tragically killed in a car accident, the club took on the mission of encouraging healthy lifestyles through spirituality and the embodiment of SuAnne's ideals.

The U. S. military has attracted many young Sioux men and women into their services. This began with World War I, even before they were declared citizens of the United States.

during the winter months, such as the New Year's Wacipi, held throughout the different reservations to celebrate the beginning of the new year according to the European calendar. (Traditionally, the Lakota new year began with the advent of the spring season and the returning of the thunders. This is still observed with a ceremony welcoming back the thunders.) Sinte Gleska University holds their annual Founder's Day Wacipi during the first weekend of February. Families may choose to have honoring ceremonies for family members at the powwows. These ceremonies could include the Hunka, where the family publicly announces a child's given Lakota name or recognizes a family member's special accomplishments.

Usually a powwow committee is selected from the year before to plan and oversee the gathering. When each committee member's term is completed, that person's family has the responsibility of feeding everyone else; the family usually has an "honoring" as well, where food and gifts are given to everyone in attendance.

The cultural aspects of the giveaway have been adapted from historical times. In the past, when an important event was to take place, all the people were invited. The host family would prepare giveaway items well in advance of the event. Giveaway items included horses, quilled and beaded items, tanned hides, and clothing. Plenty of food was prepared, because it was better to have more than not enough. The idea was to feed and give to the needy, elderly, and the orphans.

Today's giveaway still consists of providing the meal for the gathered people, but the giveaway items have changed. Although star quilts are made by family members or purchased from other Lakota women, the majority of the giveaway items—blankets, clothing, towels, and kitchen wares—are purchased. The idea of giving to the needy, elderly, and the orphans rarely or no longer exists.

Basketball is second to the powwow in bringing people together on the reservations. This sport is a culture in itself for the Sioux people. Traditionally, the Sioux entertained themselves by competing with each other through hand games and other friendly competition. When many of these pastimes were banned along with the religious practices, people had to sneak around for their entertainment. When basketball was introduced on the reservation in the 1960s, it gave them another option.

When the Oglala Community School, now Pine Ridge High School, varsity basketball team won the right to compete in the state Class B basketball tournament, family members clustered around their radios to listen as the team won the South Dakota title. Since then, Indian high school teams from the across the state of South Dakota made many more trips to the State A tournament and won several more titles.

The Lakota Nation Invitational (LNI) Basketball Tournament is held annually in mid-December in Rapid City, South Dakota. High school Indian basketball teams from across South Dakota participate with other non-Indian teams. It has become an intertribal gathering, a time to socialize and share with the relatives from across the state. Tribal meetings and educational conferences are also scheduled during this time.

Tribal hand games have been revived and are included as part of the activities of the powwow and at educational conferences. The Teca Wacipi, elementary and secondary school dance clubs of the reservation, and the American Indian Higher Education Consortium (AIHEC) have also included hand games competition. Friendly competition is alive and well among the Sioux Nation.

Vanessa Shortbull, born on the Pine Ridge Reservation, was the first American Indian Miss South Dakota at the Miss America Pageant in Atlantic City in September 2002.

Chapter 6

Contemporary Arts and Culture

One Saturday in September 2002, Pine Ridge Reservation residents were glued to their television screens as they watched the Miss America Pageant. A sense of pride prevailed as mothers told their daughters to pay attention as they waited to get a glimpse of Miss South Dakota among the other Miss America contestants parading down the runway. Miss South Dakota was Vanessa Shortbull, born in Pine Ridge village on the Pine Ridge Reservation, and the daughter of Thomas and Darlene Shortbull. She made South Dakota history as the first American Indian Miss South Dakota, breaking long-existing racial and cultural barriers. She represented the Sioux Nation with dignity.

Vanessa's family had moved to Rapid City, South Dakota, when she was a small child. She attended St. Thomas More High School, and then went

This beaded leather ball with designs of hands and horses was made by Chief Charles Eagle, Oglala Lakota, July 1993. It is in the Heritage Center of the Red Cloud Mission, Pine Ridge Reservation, South Dakota.

on to the University of South Dakota in Vermillion; she graduated in May 2002 with a bachelor of arts degree in political science. Although her parents were a great influence in her life, she was also greatly inspired by her grandmother, a strong, independent woman who never dwelled on the difficulties of life on the reservation.

Vanessa's talent was ballet, which she performed for the talent competition during the Miss America Pageant. Her love for dance, particularly ballet, came after seeing the beauty and gracefulness of another American Indian ballerina, Maria Tallchief, of the Osage tribe. When she first began her ballet lessons, Vanessa felt she was terrible, had no rhythm, and lacked coordination, but with perseverance and the encouragement of her family, her performance improved and she flourished.

Vanessa's Lakota heritage was her strength as she was growing up. The culture was always within her household. She has a strong bond with her mother and grandmother, and wherever she is, she communicates with them on her cell phone.

She said of the Miss America Pageant: "Looking at this breathtakingly huge auditorium and walking down the runway, I said, 'This is a once-in-a-lifetime experience.'" She savored the moment. Her words of advice to other Lakota youth—and youth in general—"Sometimes life may throw you to the ground, but pick yourself up and continue. And most importantly, believe in yourself!" Vanessa's future plans include attending law school; eventually, she hopes to seek public office within the state of South Dakota.

Like many other young Lakota individuals, Vanessa can dream and then make those dreams a reality. Contemporary Lakota culture and art is no longer limited to crafts, nor is it male or female dominated as it was in the past. Lakota art and culture is whatever you do as a Lakota individual—your own self-expression in a particular art form.

Traditional art, however, was divided into the female form and the male form. The women created their art in the form of beadwork and quillwork

A Sioux beaded purse, made in 1890, is part of the Red Cloud Mission Heritage Center collection.

Quillwork is a traditional art especially prized by collectors. Due to the difficulty and tediousness of the work, not many people practice this craft today. These splendid moccasins combine both quill and bead work.

Dream Art

The Ogala Sioux have a sacred tradition in which "Double Woman" (twins) came in a woman's dream to teach her the use of quills. The dreamer taught other women how to use quills, and quillworkers societies were formed. Feasts and gift giving were part of the quillworkers' meetings. Today, only a few Oceti Sakowin women continue this beautiful and ancient tradition. Their rare artwork is most highly valued.

on clothing, while the men created theirs in the form of drawing. Both told stories of family, adventure, and important events. Today, there are females who draw and create paintings and males who do beadwork and quillwork. This gender division has disappeared as a result of economic reasons; you create what the public is willing to buy.

Contemporary prominent artists who express themselves on canvas include Arthur Amiotte, Martin Red Bear, Vic Runnels, and Del Iron Cloud, and many others too numerous to mention.

Many contemporary women still continue producing beadwork and quillwork the same way they were taught by their mothers, grandmothers, or other female relatives. Quillwork is the oldest female art form, revealed to selected women through a dream in which they

Quillwork

This is an ancient Sioux art, a form of fine art long before European traders brought glass beads into America. Pieces of quillwork art over two hundred years old have been found in the Plains area. After the 1800s, beads replaced quills for many artists.

This decorative art uses porcupine quills, which are round, hollow tubes. Quills were used for trade and decoration. They were flattened and colored with vegetable dyes. Each group of the Oceti Sakowin had its own special dyes that were used to color quills. The western Sioux were known for their red, yellow, and black colors:

- Buffalo berry was used to make red dye.
- Wild sunflower or coneflower petals were boiled with cattail roots to make yellow dye.
- A black color was produced from wild grapes.

Quilt Making

Owinja means "quilt" in the Lakota dialect. Sioux star quilts are a fine art form much sought after by collectors. A single star dominates most Oceti Sakowin quilts. The star is made of small diamond-shaped patches sewn together in eight sections. When these sections are joined together, the eight-sided star is formed.

Early buffalo robe designs inspired the star. (Mission schools were teaching quilting while white hunters were exterminating the buffalo.) The morning star is an important symbol in Oceti Sakowin ceremonies. It represents the sacred directions and immortality. At funerals, a star quilt is draped behind the casket. Today, star quilts are one of the most valued gifts of the Sioux people. Star quilts are considered a necessary gift for newly married couples.

The girl in the middle of this powwow procession wears a single eight-pointed star, typical of Oceti Sakowin quilts. It represents the sacred directions.

Beadwork

Today's Oceti Sakowin beadwork evolved from traditional quillwork, an Indian invention, practiced only in North America. The materials and designs of quillwork were gradually abandoned as the art of beading became popular, since beading is easier and quicker. Sioux women acquired pony beads from European traders in the 1700s. They began to make the old quill designs with beadwork, adding for the first time the colors blue and white. Sioux artists were able to make fancier patterns than they were able to with stiff, vegetable-dyed porcupine quills. Sioux women beaded geometrical designs growing out of ancient traditions. Today's Oceti Sakowin beadwork combines artistic inspiration from both Native and non-Native cultures.

were visited by the Double Woman. The dreamer would make a decision whether to become adept in the arts, either using her hands to create beautiful pieces or using her voice to create music and song for people to hear. The woman's relatives always hoped she would choose the arts and a hardworking life; the other choice would have meant laziness and lewdness.

In addition to the beadwork and quillwork, some Sioux women today are skilled in star quilt making. This is considered a very contemporary art form, because the women began doing this after they were introduced to fabric and learned how to sew. That star is a common shape in Lakota quilts, representing the Lakota connection to the sky and the star world. Star quilts are most commonly used as special gifts.

Music and dance are other areas of self-expression. Indigenous is a

Quilts are artwork that can be worn for powwows or other special occasions.

Powwows provide opportunity for all ages to celebrate their American Indian cultures.

Jeff Bailey, Lakota Sioux, and James Horner, Kiowa (from right to left), in their regalia at the powwow on the National Mall, Washington DC, September 2002.

Kyle Keller of the Pine Ridge Thorpes leaps high to pull down a rebound over Red Cloud's Calvin Miner. High school basketball on the Great Plains Indian reservations is a culture in itself.

contemporary rock group of young Nakota tribal members from the Yankton Sioux Reservation in southeastern South Dakota. The group has been making its way around the country performing for the general population. Floyd Westerman, Dakota tribal member from the Sisseton-Wahpeton Sioux Tribe in northwestern South Dakota, has been a popular singer for many years. Buddy Red Bow, deceased Oglala tribal member from the Pine Ridge Reservation, was also a contemporary singer whose music is still heard on the local Indian radio station. All of these contemporary performers and singers have incorporated a distinct cultural flavor into their music.

The Washington Post *has referred to Russell Means as "One of the biggest, baddest, meanest, angriest, most famous American Indian activists of the late twentieth century."*

Chapter 7

Contributions to the World

"One of the biggest, baddest, meanest, angriest, most famous American Indian activists of the late twentieth century," said the *Washington Post* review of *Where White Men Fear to Tread*, Russell Means' autobiography written with Marvin J. Wolf. In the 1970s, Russell Means became notorious for defending the rights of American Indians across the United States as a member of the American Indian Movement (AIM).

Although his early life was spent on the Pine Ridge Reservation, the Means family moved to California for employment opportunities, and there he first experienced racism. As a young man, he returned to South Dakota but eventually ended up in Cleveland, Ohio.

While organizing the Cleveland Indian Center, he first met members of

Radio station KILI on Pine Ridge Reservation in South Dakota broadcasts current issues in the Lakota and English languages.

the Minnesota American Indian Movement at a National Urban Indian Organization conference in San Francisco. Their meeting was not love at first sight; they did not agree with one another on several issues. Some time after this first meeting, however, AIM members contacted Means requesting his support at a meeting in Detroit to confront the National Council of Churches. He had impressed them with his eloquent speaking abilities.

Here he was formally introduced to the American Indian Movement. Someone handed him an AIM pamphlet that quoted Chief Joseph of the Nez Perce on the front cover:

> Let me be a free man, free to travel, free to stop, free to work, free to trade where I choose, free to choose my own teachers, free to follow the religion of my fathers, free to talk, think, and act for myself—and I will obey every law or submit to the penalty.

Means was hooked from that moment. He committed himself with passion to the cause of justice for the American Indian.

All the Sioux tribes face internal problems, problems with the states in which they reside, and also with the federal government at times. Unity will be necessary for future prosperity in the face of adversity.

Another recent development that called for South Dakota tribal people to unite with non-Indian ranchers and environmentalists was the DM&E Railroad's proposal to build a rail line from the Wyoming coal mines in the Powder River area across the western to the eastern end of South Dakota.

In Russell's words, "AIM had its own axiom: When we chose to fight, *we* would pick the time and the battlefield. Because we knew we were right, we took heart in the justness of our cause and proceeded straight ahead in whatever we did without fear, certain that nothing bad could befall us."

In 1978, following The Longest Walk to Washington, D.C., to protest anti-Indian legislation, Russell Means began serving his time in the South Dakota State Penitentiary for defending the rights of his people. Two years later, the South Dakota legislature repealed the law he had been convicted of breaking. In January 2003, almost twenty-five years later, outgoing Republican Governor William Janklow of South Dakota granted Russell a pardon.

AIM's movement of courage and self-empowerment paved the way for many more individuals and tribal groups to pursue tribal, state, and national legislation regarding Indian treaty rights, human rights, and environmental issues. Women also joined ranks with the men as they pursued issues that directly affected their families and environment. Women of All Red Nations (WARN) exposed and opposed *genocide* through *sterilization* of American Indian women by government-operated Indian Health Service hospitals during the 1980s. Many of these movements brought issues to the forefront and caused tribal governments to rethink and change procedures.

Tribal governments are not immune from corruption—and Native activists have also taken up the cause to expose corruption within tribal government. One Oglala tribal member, Charmaine Whiteface, saw corruption and questioned it three months into her term as tribal treasurer in 1988; she was suspended as a result of her courage and threatened with *impeachment*. Her position remained in limbo until her term eventually expired in 1990. Her book *Testimony of the Innocent* is an account of her experience. Today, she is a freelance writer, actively involved with environmental issues affecting tribal members. She is currently assisting in the development of language for the Grasslands/Wilderness Bill.

A *grassroots* group of elderly people has united on the Pine Ridge Reservation to form the Gray Eagle Society. Their purpose is to advise Sioux gatherings; they have sometimes aired concerns about current issues over the local radio station in their native language. They have stood firmly in support of issues that would benefit their people and have opposed issues that would harm them.

Another grassroots group united in the 1980s to oppose *zeolites* mining on the northeast end of the Pine Ridge Reservation. The mines would have meant millions of dollars in annual revenue for one of the poorest counties in the United States. Studies revealed that the particular type of zeolites located on the reservation was not *carcinogenic*, but the peoples' value of respect for Unci Maka (Grandmother Earth) was stronger than their need for wealth; the mining never occurred. The undisturbed zeolite deposit on the Pine Ridge Reservation is the second largest in the world.

Another environmental issue that affects all the Oceti Sakowin tribes is the Missouri River. The Sioux have long held treaty rights to the Missouri River, but because of early federal legislation, dams were built, flooding tribal reservation land and burial grounds. Tribal members had to be relocated. Most recently, more federal legislation has surfaced with the introduction of the Wildlife Habitat Mitigation Act regarding the Missouri, causing a slight rift between the tribes. South Dakota Senator Tom Daschle separated the Sioux tribes with his claims that only those tribes located along the river could make decisions regarding its usage. The Cheyenne River Sioux Tribe and the Lower Brule Tribe supported Senator Daschle's legislation. The rest of the Sioux tribes claim the decision should have involved all tribes who signed the 1868 treaty. The act is currently held up by pending lawsuits.

Currently, a federally funded program called the Mni Wiconi Project is piping Missouri River water to some of the reservations. Grassroots groups have been involved in this water issue as well, journeying on numerous occasions to the state capitol in Pierre to protest. When a vote was taken in the early 1990s to decide whether or not to accept the proposed Mni Wiconi Project on the Pine Ridge Reservation, tribal members voted not to accept it—but the project went forward anyway with the support of the Tribal Council. The Mni Wiconi Project was to provide water to the Red Shirt Table community on the western edge of the Pine Ridge Reservation, but pipelines to off-reservation counties and reservation communities who already had water were laid first. Skeptical residents watched as the pipeline was laid up to their front doors, and rumors ran rampant that eventually private wells were to be capped and everyone would be forced to use the piped water and be charged for usage. This project and many others conflict with traditional beliefs that nobody owns the natural resources. Instead, the earth and its resources were placed here for people to use in a respectful manner.

Another recent development that called for South Dakota tribal people to unite with non-Indian ranchers and environmentalists was the Dakota Minnesota & Eastern (DM&E) Railroad's proposal to build a rail line from the Wyoming coal mines in the western Powder River area across the state to the eastern end of South Dakota. The proposed line would have crossed tribal land on the reservation, disturbing the land and native wildlife. Many tribal people, elderly non-Indian ranchers, and environmentalists united and called themselves the CIA (Cowboy Indian Alliance); together they spoke in opposition to the proposal. This proposed project is currently held up by pending lawsuits.

The struggle for protection of tribal treaty rights, human rights, and environmental rights is an unending battle. Many times, the individuals who fight on behalf of these issues receive little or no recognition—and yet their scrupulous research and publication of their findings brings public awareness. As Charmaine Whiteface has said, "Once the public becomes aware of the issue and begins to take action, I move on to another issue." An activist is always one step ahead, looking for issues that could harm people or the environment.

The Black Hills continue to be a source of spiritual strength and inspiration for today's Sioux people.

Chapter 8

Challenges for Today, Hopes for the Future

At the first class meeting of Seminar in Contemporary Indian Issues, the students filed slowly into the classroom. The eighteen students ranged in age from their early twenties to early fifties. The group was comprised of a former tribal president, a police officer, an IHS employee, high school Lakota language and culture teachers, tribal employees, and young full-time students. The first topic of discussion was the definitions of "sovereignty" and "nationhood." Are tribes *sovereign nations*? To what extent are they sovereign? The group agreed that the tribes fit the criteria for nationhood. Most tribes had a body of people bound together by a common language, cultural beliefs, a land base, and a capacity to govern themselves.

The U.S. government signed its last treaty with the Sioux tribes in 1868, giving them a formal recognition as peers, which should have made them

A sign and wreath on Pine Ridge Reservation in South Dakota reminds people not to drink and drive.

fully sovereign nations. Recognition became permanent unless that tribe ceased to exist or lost the criteria for nationhood. Tribes were nations but "quasi-sovereign," because the U.S. government kept them in a state of dependency. Today, all tribal members need to be educated on the legal status of tribes within the United States.

Red Cloud showed foresight when he negotiated and signed the 1868 Fort Laramie Treaty, which left the Sioux tribes with a huge land base to live on. In 1876, after gold was discovered in the Black Hills, the United States tried unsuccessfully to purchase the Black Hills—but the Sioux tribes never sold the Black Hills, claiming this land held great religious significance for them. The United States persisted and set aside the money for its one-sided agreement, money that the Sioux have not touched to this day. Red Cloud's words in response to the Black Hills Agreement of 1876 have haunted the generations that followed: the Black Hills, Red Cloud said, were only a loan to the United States for seven generations. It is now the responsibility of the seventh generation to renegotiate the Black Hills issue. This issue is an important one for the future of the Sioux people.

All the Sioux tribes have become considerably educated through the U.S. educational systems. The Sioux can proudly boast of their doctors, lawyers, nurses, teachers, college professors, administrators, and businesspeople. These well-educated tribal members began to assert their sovereign rights once they realized that they could make decisions for themselves, and they had the right to question the federal government. The state has no legal power on the Indian reservations; only the federal government does in some

Prairie Wind Casino in the Pine Ridge Reservation, South Dakota, is one economic venture attempting to produce more wealth for the Oglala Lakota.

Casinos improve the finances of many Sioux tribes.

criminal cases. Federal funding goes directly to tribal governments. Tribal members observe and are subject to state laws when off the reservation.

A controversial political issue affecting many tribes, including the Sioux, is gaming. In 1988, Congress passed Public Law 100-497, the Indian Gaming Regulatory Act (IGRA). Today, many of the Sioux tribes own and operate casinos as a means to generate revenue for tribal government operations, employment opportunities, and to support the general welfare of their tribal members. Tribal members receive monthly **per capita** payments from gaming facilities. The Shakopee Mdewakantonwan Dakota Sioux Tribe, with a small tribal enrollment, owns the Mystic Lake Casino located near Minneapolis-St. Paul, Minnesota. As a result, they are financially wealthier than other Sioux tribes.

Economic and social conditions on other reservations are deplorable, however. The reservation unemployment has ranged from 45 percent to as high as 80 percent. Alcoholism and drug abuse runs rampant. The positive side of Indian gaming is that it creates some jobs and reduces some dependence on social welfare programs, but it hasn't solved all the Sioux's social and economic problems. Indian gaming near tribal communities brings its own potential problems, including the possibility of compulsive addiction, increased alcohol and drug abuse, crime, and neglect and abuse of children. The opportunities for theft, embezzlement, and criminal infiltration exist as well. Many Sioux feared the loss of cultural integrity within the surrounding Indian community as a result of gaming.

Indian gaming has created a new issue over Indian sovereignty. According to the treaties, since the casinos are located on federal trust land, the state has no legal authority. Some states do not like that the tribes are exempt from paying taxes and have reduced state regulatory control. IGRA subsequently stipulated that Class III gaming could be offered only through a tribal-state compact. Compacts have given states the power to exercise some control over Indian gaming.

Another contemporary issue has been over cultural property rights and intellectual property rights. All cultures possess knowledge connected to their spirituality. How does one protect itself from intellectual and cultural exploitation?

At a college science conference held in the spring of 1999, an Indian *geneticist* served as one of the panelists. In a private conversation, he shared information regarding pharmaceutical companies' actions in taking tribal plants and herbs for analysis of medicinal properties. Once a *patent* is placed on these medicines, they will no longer belong to the tribes. He believed that the tribes should establish laws to protect themselves from such acts. However, the tribes have yet to take action on this matter.

Language is another controversial issue affecting many of the Sioux

---

Quasi-Sovereign

This is the term used by the U.S. government to refer to Indian tribes. It means they are self-ruling but only partly independent. The federal government recognizes that tribes have the right to make their own laws and choose their own leaders, but the government insists that the tribes' decisions cannot interfere with the interests of the United States or deny Indian citizens their U.S. constitutional rights.

Angie Reyes is a Lakota tribal member and her husband is of Mexican American descent. They own and operate this Mexican restaurant in Kyle, South Dakota, on the Pine Ridge Reservation. Small businesses are important in reservation economic development.

tribes. Although Christianity and the boarding schools nearly destroyed the traditional Sioux language, it has survived. Language is vital because the culture *is* in the language; traditional ceremonies cannot be performed, nor can certain ideas be expressed, if the language is gone. Many middle-aged and elderly tribal members still speak their native language, but it is on the verge of extinction. As long as the Sioux people practice their ceremonies, however, the language will remain.

Recently, a Midwest university was invited to one of the elementary schools on the reservation to assist in the *revitalization* of the Lakota language. The situation soon became a question of cultural and intellectual rights. The university wanted a contract that would allow them to develop a Lakota language curriculum, develop CD-ROMs, and essentially be in charge of the project. The question was unclear on the copyright issue: Who would own the language?

Health is another issue of concern on the reservations. The Sioux tribes were once a healthy people because of their *nomadic* lifestyle and their dependence on wild game, vegetables, and fruits. After a century of a *sedentary* lifestyle and dependence on government commodities high in fat and starches, however, the Sioux's health has declined. *Diabetes* has reached *epidemic* proportions on many of the reservations and has challenged people to change their current lifestyles. Programs that actively promote awareness of and educate people on the prevention of the disease are prevalent. These programs send outreach workers to do home visits, and they touch the lives of many other people over the local radio station. They have successfully prompted many people to exercise and change their diet.

Alcoholism remains a challenge on the reservation. Alcohol was first

Signs on public buildings are one evidence that the Lakota dialect has survived, despite attempts to destroy it through Christianity and boarding schools.

introduced to the Sioux people when they came into contact with the traders between 1825 and 1835—and it has remained a social problem ever since. Alcohol is prohibited on the Pine Ridge Reservation, but the sale of alcohol is allowed in a small Nebraska town located two miles south of the Pine Ridge village. Tribal members have protested against the sale of alcohol to tribal members, but thus far, nothing has been done.

All the Sioux tribes have internal problems, problems with the states in which they reside, and also with the federal government—but despite these problems, they have survived for centuries. And they will continue to survive, adapting as they live from day to day. Their spirituality has remained strong and has served as their foundation.

High school girls cheer their team at the Lakota Nation Invitational Basketball tournament. Sioux teens need to be well educated in order to understand the issues facing them, and strong in their own culture as well. In this way, the Sioux people will continue to thrive.

A new day is dawning for the Sioux people—and they face the future with courage, hope, and dignity.

Achievement

The achievements of my people unroll behind me from the misty dawn of time. Measured against them and against the lives of all who came before me, my own span on this earth is no more than the arc of a single arrow. I don't know how long or how high the Archer intends me to soar, but so far it has been a thrilling, awesome, magnificent flight.

—Russell Means in *Where White Men Fear to Tread*

The Seventh Generation

Many Indian nations see the number seven as having special significance. For instance, the Oceti Sakowin are the People of the Seven Council Fires and the Lakota speak of seven Original People. Many American Indians recognize a great responsibility to those who will come after them, down to the seventh generation. This means that a person's behavior is guided by thinking about the effects of their actions on those who will come after him or her.

The Sioux have many hopes for the future:

• that the current generations will continue the fight to protect the legacy of their ancestors through defending treaty rights, human rights, and environmental rights.
• that the young people will be well-educated in the outside world in order to understand the issues that concern them.
• that this generation and future generations will display traditional leadership qualities—courage, respect, generosity, wisdom, and humility.

Perhaps the most important hope is the advice of the elders: "carry the people in your heart."

Further Reading

Black Elk. *Black Elk Speaks: Being the Life Story of a Holy Man of the Oglala Sioux*. Lincoln: Bison Books, 2000.

Brown, Dee. *Bury My Heart at Wounded Knee*. New York: Henry Holt, 1991.

Crow Dog, Leonard and Richard Erdoes. *Crow Dog: Four Generations of Sioux Medicine Men*. New York: HarperCollins, 1995.

Crow Dog, Mary. *Lakota Woman*. New York: HarperCollins, 1990.

Gagnon, Gregory and Karen White Eyes. *Pine Ridge Reservation Yesterday and Today*. Sioux Falls. S.D.: Badlands Natural History Association, 1992.

Means, Russell. *Where White Men Fear to Tread: The Autobiography of Russell Means*. New York: St. Martin's Press, 1995.

For More Information

American Indian Movement Grand Governing Council
www.aimovement.org/

Canku Ota (Many Paths) An Online Newsletter Celebrating Native America
www.turtletrack.org/

KILI Radio—the Voice of the Lakota Nation
www.lakotamall.com/kili/

Pine Ridge Reservation
www.pineridgerez.net/

Russell Means Treaty Production Homepage
www.russellmeans.com/

Publisher's Note:

The Web sites listed on this page were active at the time of publication. The publisher is not responsible for Web sites that have changed their address or discontinued operation since the date of publication. The publisher will review and update the Web sites upon each reprint.

Glossary

accredited: Having met the necessary requirements to grant degrees.

activist: Someone who works on behalf of a cause.

anthropologists: People who study the science of human beings.

assimilation: Changing people's beliefs and culture to make them like others.

ballot box tampering: A method of manipulating an election by improperly handling the votes cast.

carcinogenic: Something that produces cancer.

constitution: The rules, laws, and principles guiding a government or group.

criteria: A set of standards by which decisions or judgments are made.

curriculum: The courses offered by an educational institution.

diabetes: A disease caused by inadequate production or use of insulin.

dung: Manure; excrement of an animal.

epidemic: Affecting a large number of people within a community.

fluidity: The quality of being able to flow, to change as necessary.

geneticist: Someone who studies heredity.

genocide: The systematic destruction of a racial, political, or cultural group.

grassroots: Political movements that begin with common people, rather than politicians or businesses.

homesteaders: People who claimed a tract of property from U.S. public land simply by filing a record and living on it.

impeachment: Removal of a person from political office, usually because that person has proven to be dishonest or has not fulfilled the duties of the office.

incumbent: The person currently holding an elected office.

Manifest Destiny: A policy of expansion based on the belief that it is for the good of the people being "taken over."

medicine men: Priestly healers.

nomadic: Moving from place to place.

patent: A document guaranteeing an inventor the exclusive right to make, use, or sell an invention for a set number of years.

per capita: For each person.

petroglyphs: Carvings or inscriptions on a rock.

pictographs: Symbols belonging to a pictorial graphic system.

Presbyterian: A form of Protestant Christian belief.

primary election: An election held generally to reduce the number of candidates running for a particular office in the general election.

Protestants: Christians who are not Catholic and who emphasize the importance of the Bible rather than ceremonies.

reservation: A tract of public land set aside for use by a particular group.

revitalization: The process of giving new life to something or someone.

sedentary: Something done in a sitting or inactive position.

smear campaign: A campaign practice of saying bad things about the opposing candidate.

solstice: One of the two points at which the distance from the ecliptic and its celestial equator are the greatest.

sovereign nations: Independent countries with the right to make their own laws, choose their own rulers, and defend their own interests.

sterilization: The practice of making someone unable to produce an offspring.

underground: Existing outside the establishment.

zeolites: Minerals used for chemical and farming processes.

Index

Biographies

Karen LoneHill is chairperson of the Lakota Studies Department at Oglala Lakota College. In addition to teaching Lakota language, history, and culture, she participates in traditional Lakota cultural ceremonies. Her research interests include the history of the Porcupine district of Pine Ridge Reservation. She has done extensive curriculum development in Native American Studies.

Martha McCollough received her bachelor's and master's degrees in anthropology at the University of Alaska-Fairbanks, and she now teaches at the University of Nebraska. Her areas of study are contemporary Native American issues, ethnohistory, and the political and economic issues that surround encounters between North American Indians and Euroamericans.

Benjamin Stewart, a graduate of Alfred University, is a freelance photographer and graphic artist. He traveled across North America to take the photographs included in this series.